L

A

David Cobb was born and raised in Harrow and was a Life Guards trooper before taking a German degree at Bristol University. His working life has been spent in education, in Britain, Germany, Thailand, the Middle East and Africa. In 1973 he joined a publisher of EFL courses, but in 1985 became a victim of what he vaguely understands to have been "market economy forces", and has since then worked as a freelance. His schoolbooks are used in many parts of the world, particularly in countries where there are problems with currency exchange.

He has been writing memento mori since the age of 15, and haiku and senryu since the age of 51.

He now lives in a rural part of Essex.

A Leap in the Light

David Cobb

EQUINOX PRESS

Acknowledgements: Many of this selection of haiku and senryu have appeared previously in the following publications: (in Britain) Iron, The Rialto, The Haiku Quarterly, Quartos, Candelabrum, Buddhism Now; (in Canada) Daybreak, Haiku Canada; (in Japan) Ko, Mainichi; (and in the USA) Brussels Sprout, Modern Haiku.

To the editors of these I give my thanks for their support, as to several friends, especially James Kirkup (who incidentally discovered "Thingland" before me), Joan Giroux, James Hackett, and Dee Evetts. I am also delighted with Charlotte Smith's sensitive drawings.

British Library Cataloguing in Publication Data
Cobb, David *1926* -
A leap in the light
I. Title
821.914

ISBN 0-9517103-0-3

Published in 1991 by Equinox Press, Sinodun House, Shalford, Braintree, Essex CM7 5HN

Design and Typeset by Ray Owen

Printed by Higham Press Ltd, Shirland Derby DE5 6BP

Orders in North America to: PO Box 313, La Honda, CA 94020, USA

SPRING, EAST ANGLIA

shimmer of fish

without any motion

through a film of ice

the torrent passes

in soft slow ripples

through the gills of fish

first day of spring -
the starling wipes its beak
against a thorn

on the misty pear
all of a sudden buds
burst into sparrows

the tide coming in -
footprints on the salt flats
pointing out to sea

’flu convalescent
craning for apple buds
a flight of finches

losing the blossom
from the cherry, gaining
a lawn of petals

house for sale:
in its mailbox robins' eggs
cold under letters

arms round a fuchsia
he stands at the greenhouse door
sniffing for frost

with the wind

against the wind

the smell of rape

delicate spider

inches

past the grimy pane

SUMMER, EAST ANGLIA

shirts off
labourers posturing
with flexed tattoos

red admiral
on a snag of rusted wire
quite motionless

on the putting green
careful to miss no hole -
a bumble bee

a cloudless sky -
painters stretch ladders
to their farthest rungs

a moment between
lighthouse flashes -
cold smell of fish

under the lily

pungent as never before

the staling of cats

with urgency

the snail is pursuing

a green lettuce

summer, east anglia

between shrew and cat
a dandelion clock
about to go off

abseiling spider
accelerating
with a drop of rain

in deep blue sea
bounce of mother and baby
dumping a nappy

beach picnic -

little crabs' sanctuary

under the basket

in the shade, cool drinks:

a sudden scalding splash

of butterfly

old gardener

back that doesn't bend, nosing

night-scented stocks

the sweating gardener
has opened his armpits
to the honeysuckle

between the legs
of the grazing cow
blue sky

stepping stones:
in the middle of next stride
a wasp at rest

summer, east anglia

in its tick of life

the fly hovers for an age

above one lily

a wasp is browsing

the complete works of Wordsworth

on its way to jam

summer, east anglia

every movement
the grasshopper makes -
a leap in the light

the bee enters
its buzz
in the foxglove

between dusk and dawn
sandal-prints on the shore
have turned into boots

choreography
for midsummer picnicking -
by thunderbugs

the speeding ball
before I close my hand
caught by the sun

stooking wheat -
within the dew-damp sheaves
thistle dust

bolting rabbit -
the last few dewdrops spill
from lupin stems

gathering dusk
        black slug gleaming
        out of dewy grass

the rising moon
full on my nape
the breath of a moth

late summer breeze -
leaves of my book turning
before they are read

the end of summer -
putting the clocks back
but a single hour

AUTUMN, EAST ANGLIA

old briar scent

crosses the twilit garden

to the scion rose

dahlia petals

fall and reassemble

in a cobweb form

autumn, east anglia

some of the seed is
finding earth in daylight, some
where night has fallen

muck-spreaders:
corners of mouths smelling
of cigarettes

evening chill -

mosquitoes tap their beaks

on double glass

buzzard's plumes

all out of place

on the leaf-bare tree

the farmer leaves
the scarecrow
minding dung

no space on the path
and in the air adrift
red maple leaves

on the pip of noon
robin poop on the last
rose of November

autumn, east anglia

wind on my hand
riffling the pile of leaves
for the windbell's tongue

pear leaves fall:
a landscape starts to form
between the branches

scarecrow in the wind
bowing bowing then toppling
on its feet again

a morning for Keats:

below the mist a limbo

-dancing weasel

WINTER, EAST ANGLIA

beside dead leaves
the husk of a ladybird
vibrant with colour

with every spade-spit
the sexton buries the corpse
of another worm

on weather-worn stones
refreshing epitaphs
unending rain

February frost -
numb feet tingle
on the molehill crusts

ice extends
to where the snow begins
to turn to ice

winter, east anglia

a night of fever
oblivious of ice
crusting the panes

snow forecast, but
the rooks still beat a path
upwind, to the north

curiosity
something the cat lacks, chipping
frost on its cack

winter, east anglia

cracked sandals
in the porch since summer
filling with snow

on the stroke of noon
the snow-gown of the cypress
is turning to rags

from dis-hedged roads
farmers are tractoring home
an acreage of snow

like all true snowmen
this one began as a small boy
rolling a daruma

arms in a hug
the snowman eases his limbs
beneath the lawn

c

RED LETTER DAYS

New Year's market -
dribble freezes
on the haddocks' jaws

on my desk a pile
of unslit envelopes - one
my pension claim

a lull in winter -
the sexton pegs the sunshine
into portions

Twelfth Night -
postponing the climb-down
with the tinsel star

birthday dinner -
lid of the ricepot
bubbling over

Good Friday mass -
ants at the lychgate
with an apple core

an Easter squall -

roses clinging to trees

with all their thorns

carnival day:

in my begging tin, perfume

from a stranger's rose

the altar cluttered

just a few petals

on the chancel floor

headlights pick out
after our celebration
sorrel in seed

at the air mail box
flying everywhere -
flakes of snow

last night of Christmas -
dry spruce-needle barbs
in brand-new socks

TRAVELLERS

a riot of clothes

on the gipsy washing line -

uniformly frosted

before he washes

he scrubs his romany chest

with scoops of mist

the shaggy pony
tethered to shadows
keeps its head well down

a frosty dawn -
curtains drawn early
to display cut-glass

porcelain hoard
in the caravan window -
a show of white backs

the gipsy queen

is massaging her jaws

with a celery stick

"SPECiALiSTS"

a scrawl on the trailer says

"iN FENCiNG"..........

NEWS FROM THINGLAND

Trafalgar Square:

the pigeon man feeds millet

to my lover's hand

migrating swallows

sharing slack cable

with a fax machine

November Friday:

in a dockyard unmanned cranes

bow into fog

black refuse bags

stacked behind the square

with London's leaves

we’re here, love, again

in this café where your fly

has no time for mine

patting her hound

the English lady pincers

an éclair

in a double bed

alone - waking
diagonally

on tatami

my Japanese character

might be 大

(pronounced 'dai',
meaning 'largeness')

but if I went west

maybe I'd think I was

a capital X

outside the window
a voice awakens someone
          using my name

my neighbour's busy
shovelling last night's bedroom
into a barrow

the cypress is down -
where will the dove coo now
at dusk, at dawn?

satellite dishes

brimming with moonshine:

lowering sky

outside, the cold:

muffle of postman's mittens

on the letter-flap

MOMENTS FROM ADJACENT PLACES

this unwalked garden
of derelict monuments -
then cherry pips!

old Roman stalls -
a cat slinks paw by paw
to the sunniest seat

lads by the castle wall
making their soccer goals -
sarcophagii

in Socrates' cave
the recent campers' shit
          an ancient smell

first hint of spring -
a thin snake half emerges
to be poked with sticks

at burning noon
round the solitary tree
some headless sheep

monsoon rains

regular at five

my girl with the curse

we sweat on our bed

after each climax

the rain never stops

she applies a salve

and licks her softened lips

then buggers the heat

D

zoo for "Net Blankes" -

dizzying the railings

zebras' stripes

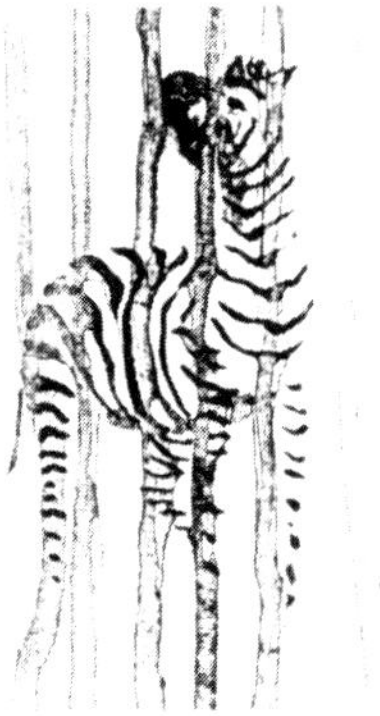

call to prayer:

the guard aligns his gun

with Mecca

in our dance she turns

from being an Eskimo

to an Inuit

spider fry -

scores of them cluster

in the Buddha's eye

siesta time -

cool in the campanile

the shadowed bells

Chiyoda-ku:

joggers run circles

round the Emperor

in Chiyoda-ku

tremors in flower-beds

          and workmen hoeing

the ryokan at last -
washing grime off our faces
at adjacent sinks

shine on her nose:
the dancer's powderpuff
mops up the moon

frontier post:

a kestrel deals with the to

and fro of the wind

old battlefield:

summer hail stinging

tumbled cairns

NOT FAR FROM HEAVEN

oppressive heat:
the toddler's piddle dries
before she can touch

boy on the sands
        using papa's sandalmarks
                as stepping stones

bulging cheeks -
a stripling pisses
in the waterfall

grammar lesson -
a pupil's tongue pops out
coral pink

last vacant room:
sliding into bed
not to wake the child

from the well at dusk
crossing the graveyard dust
the child spills nothing

LOVING CUPS

trying to capture
your escaping hair, the wind
entangles itself

Hang-gliders hover
above two lovers
circling one another

a song she knows well -
she sings it with her eyes
wide open

how odd this room is -
two of us filled it once,
one leaves it empty

sometimes just one hair
fallen in a vacant room
will not be picked up

FOR A PASSING

her careworn hands
wrinkling exactitude
into watercress

she hears her son
listening to her daughter
over her head

geriatric ward -
the cat licks the offense
of antiseptic

for a passing

at ninety she holds on
an apple in her mouth
throughout a snooze

her finger skin
perfectly mortises
the wrinkled grape

from the fever bed
immeasurably distant
tap at the door

the whole length
of the funeral route -
wisteria droops

scavenger birds
watching from the roadside
sleek-plumed cars

base of the pile
a pair of walking shoes
she never wore out

POSTSCRIPT

clock at repair:

dealing the patience cards

missing its tick